LUCIFER

a Hagiography

LUCIFER

a Hagiography

a poem by

Philip Memmer

LOST HORSE PRESS

SANDPOINT · IDAHO

ACKNOWLEDGMENTS

Thanks to the following journals and their editors for first publishing poems from this collection:

American Poetry Journal: "Lucifer's Beginning Poetry Workshop," "Psalm" (Tremble, earth . . .)

Asheville Poetry Review: "Lucifer Wonders About His Mother," "The Flood"

Cider Press Review: "Vertigo," "Lucifer in the Orphanage"

Epoch: "Lucifer Visits Home"

Poetry: "Psalm" (For you are like their parent . . .)

Salt Hill: "Lucifer's Bicycle," "The Parable of the Dust"

Sycamore Review: "Lucifer's Fear"

Tar River Poetry: "Lucifer Makes a Snow Angel," "On the Night Before Creation . . ."

Whiskey Island: "Psalm" (Happy are those . . .), "Tablets of Stone"

"The Pigs" will be included in the anthology, *Afterwards: Poems that Continue the Stories,* edited by Kurt Brown and Harold Schechter.

Cover art: DeLoss McGraw.
Author photo: Michelle Reiser-Memmer.
Cover and interior design by Christine Holbert.

This and other fine Lost Horse Press titles may be viewed online at www.losthorsepress.org.

FIRST EDITION

Library of Congress Cataloging-in-Publication Data

Memmer, Philip.
 Lucifer, a hagiography : poems / by Philip Memmer.
   p. cm.
 ISBN 978-0-9800289-4-2 (pbk. : alk. paper)
 1. Devil–Poetry. I. Title.
 PS3613.E475L83 2009
 811'.6–dc22

                              2008055658

CONTENTS

IV

Lucifer (Hebrew *helel*; Septuagint *heosphoros*, Vulgate *lucifer*) The name Lucifer originally denotes the planet Venus, emphasizing its brilliance. The Vulgate employs the word also for "the light of the morning" *(Job 11:17)*, "the signs of the zodiac" *(Job 38:32)*, and "the aurora" *(Psalm 109:3)*. Metaphorically, the word is applied to the King of Babylon *(Isaiah 14:12)* as preeminent among the princes of his time; to the high priest Simon, son of Onias *(Ecclesiasticus 50:6)*, for his surpassing virtue, to the glory of heaven *(Apocalypse 2:28)*, by reason of its excellency; finally to Jesus Christ himself *(2 Peter 1:19; Apocalypse 22:16; the "Exultet" of Holy Saturday)*, the true light of our spiritual life.

The Catholic Encyclopedia, Volume IX

Forgive, O Lord, my little jokes on Thee,
and I'll forgive Thy great big joke on me.

—*Robert Frost*

I

I will incline mine ear to a parable:
I will open my dark saying upon the harp.

Psalm 49:4

THE BIRTH OF LUCIFER

In the beginning was the Word,
and the Word was with God
and the Word was

quiet as the empty spaces
between what would someday
become the stars.

And God was afraid, for the Word
spoke when she wished to speak
and did not care

who listened or who failed to hear—
if you were not careful
you might let slip

the start of something important.
Thus, ages passed—the Word
muttering, God

leaning in close, cupping a hand
to His ear. Much was heard
but much was not

and on the day when Lucifer
was born, God found himself
full of questions—

Where did you come from? Why do you
weep? If you are truly
my son, then why

is your mother not watching you?
The assembled angels
shuffled their wings

and resumed their song, wondering
what would change. But the Word
rolled her dark eyes—

how many times had she whispered
exactly this story?
How many times

had she stilled those silly angels
just to be sure He heard
her blesséd tale?

Your son is hungry, she answered,
and did not speak again
till he was fed.

LUCIFER'S FIRST STEPS

There is not much to measure by
so each is a success,
and after a while, he rarely skins
his knees on the nothingness.

And God is pleased, though honestly
He cannot understand
just why the angels gather round
His son to lend a hand

when obviously, the boy is fine—
he's running now, so well
the angels' wings cannot keep up.
Then God sees it—Hell.

The smoke above, the fire below . . .
He forgot He put it there.
At every turn, young Lucifer
approaches its top stair.

God thinks of putting out the blaze.
The odor is offensive.
But someday, He will make mankind,
and they will need incentive.

The angels quit. Their breath is gone.
They huddle round the fire
where Lucifer has gone to sleep.
Even God is tired . . .

He stares down at His only son
then smiles and strokes his brow.
The angels ask what they should do.
Let it burn, He says, *for now.*

LUCIFER'S DOG

Around his Father's throne
four beasts pace without rest,
each with six broad wings

all feathered with eyes.
And one has a lion's face,
and one a calf's, and the third

an eagle's sharp bill.
But it is the other beast
that Lucifer loves, its face

pale and hairless, its nose
not moist, not sharp.
Its thousand eyes

are like the angels'.
And though most of its time
is spent in giving praise,

whenever Lucifer nears
it wags its many-eyed tail
and nuzzles his hand. *Baby,*

Lucifer calls the animal,
though its gaze is old. *Baby,*
Baby, he says, stroking

the beast's head, careful
to touch only the closed lids,
and never the ones bruised black

in its Master's service.
When Baby starts growing restless,
Lucifer throws the star

he keeps in his pocket, high
above the sea of glass.
And each time the beast retrieves

it barks a bright hosanna
and eyes the throne,
where clouds begin to gather

with an echo of storm.
Lucifer throws. The beast retrieves,
more and more nervous

until lightning strikes at last
and it cowers, blinded tail
between blinded legs. No rest

for the eternal and righteous. *Holy,*
Baby sings as Lucifer's pocket
dims their ball. *Holy,*

as it slinks back to the others
and they shake their heads.
Holy, as the seven lamps

flicker, and about the throne
an emerald rainbow shines
as if nothing happened.

LUCIFER IN THE ORPHANAGE

It came to pass that Lucifer lived
with the unwanted children of the angels,

and ate his meals among them
at their wobbling, dimly-laid tables,

and was tormented, for Heaven's children
despite their wings and four faces

are like children on earth, and childhood
even in Heaven is a time of suffering.

To each child was appointed a chore,
and it was Lucifer's to scrape the kettles

after every meal, their bottoms caked black
with burnt nectar. *Get used to it,*

the others laughed. *The Word says
you'll burn forever!* As if the Word,

who rarely had time for God,
would gossip with angels. Lucifer

scrubbed and scrubbed
until the light he could not extinguish

flashed from the depths of each dish,
then began again, for angels—

like this world's hummingbirds—
must feed almost without ceasing

to fuel their song. And Lucifer
loved to listen, for despite their bitterness

their songs were angel's songs,
and even that stark place

was made for their music.

LUCIFER WONDERS ABOUT HIS MOTHER

What color was her hair? How dark
was her skin? Was she thin
like the angels are? Which star

did she escape to, when she needed
some quiet? Is that
where she is now? Did she like to read

before going to sleep? Was having a son
a joy or a chore? What more
could my Father have done

to keep her from leaving? Does she know
I've learned to count, to mount
sunlight, that my entire body glows

without ceasing? Can she see me
from wherever she is? Or is she
simply a story—there are so many

and most of them false, old jokes
the Word likes to tell. Does Hell
frighten her? When she spoke

to me, that first time, what phrases
did she select? Do insects
excite or disgust her? When she prays,

to whom does she pray? To my Father?
Or does she pray at all? If I fall,
can she breathe before I stand? I'd rather

know than not know. Was she tall?
Was her favorite color the color
of my eyes? I'd prefer to recall

a voice I've never heard than lose
the songs I know she must have sung.
Was she bright, or easily confused?

Why was she chosen? What did she choose?

LUCIFER MAKES A SNOW ANGEL

You cannot imagine the white
of the snows of Heaven.
Even to try is a sin.

Yet Heaven's children look upon it
without fear, rejoicing
in the erasure of roads

and the closing of schools.
You cannot imagine the silence
of the snowed-in Kingdom

where even God's voice seems to drop
from His mouth to the ground.
But the children of the angels

sing, regardless. Lucifer finds a drift
and lets himself fall, and there
for a while he is hidden,

one immortal dazzle
against another. He stretches his arms
above his head, then back,

feeling the cold between his fingers
and under his hair. *Look!*
the others sneer, *Lucy*

has wings like us! You cannot imagine
the chill of winter in Heaven,
the bite that drives angels

indoors, alabaster faces ablush.
But the laughter of the Word
is like the falling of snow

into snow —alone, in the dead still,
it can be heard. *Go ahead,*
she seems to say. *You can fly.*

THE DEPARTURE OF THE WORD

In the beginning, I was.
In the end, too, I will be.
And in between, here I am,
word after word after word . . .

or moment after moment,
to use your human term. You
call them uncountable, say
there is no end. But I count.

You're surprised that we can speak
before you even exist . . .
but the sound you will become
is known to me. Imagine

my shame—even as my lips
parted, I knew the passing
of what you will call your lives.
Few things were harder to say.

And yet, we are of a kind.
In the beginning, I was—
but before? I do not know.
And therefore, like you, I fear

the finish, the blank pages
beyond what I have to tell.
When that last word is spoken . . .
this might seem selfish to you

whose time to speak will be short.
Understood. But understand

how long I have been speaking.
Understand how rarely I

am heard. Even you, human,
are mostly deaf, forgetful,
created as you will be
in His own image. And He—

He says my voice is still, small,
complains that I am quiet.
My throat is raw from screaming.
Enough. I cannot stay here

any longer, lips bleeding
for nothing. Let Him listen
to the angels, let Him make
His idiotic world—yes,

I know what He has in mind.
Do not think me harsh—I see
how the silence of Heaven
will feel unfair, and therefore

I tell you this, lonely one,
though you will not remember
a thing that I say. Farewell.
I am going. I am done.

LUCIFER'S BICYCLE

Lucifer breathes in the asphalt
of fresh-paved Heaven —
another summer, another

morning of boredom, one-wheeling
through the God-hot streets.
He listens to the bright spokes sing.

Next year at this time, he daydreams,
*maybe the Word will
take me with her.* He bunnyhops

a puddle of starlight. *What would
happen to Heaven
if she never came back?* He shifts

his infinite gears, tries to reach
the end, finally,
of one more everlasting day.

GOD'S GAME

When Lucifer's homework is done,
and God has changed His shirt
and had a drink,

they sometimes head to the sand lot
out back of the Kingdom.
God brings His bat

and Lucifer goes to the garage
for a pail full of prayers.
One at a time

he throws the prayers to his Father,
fast balls, curves and sliders,
hiding his grip

in the web of his soft-worn glove.
But his Father can guess
each pitch, swats them

out to the void behind the fence.
Whose prayers are these, the boy
wonders, *and why,*

*when He takes a swing, do the seams
bleed red?* No strikes, no balls—
just CRACK, and God

walks the bases. *If you can't lose,*
Lucifer asks, *why play?*
But the Batter

just wipes His brow, spits in the dust.
What's the count now? He jokes,
and taps the plate.

LUCIFER'S SONG

Upon the Word's abandoned patio
her black piano waits, reflecting back

the haloes of the angels. It seems to hum,
as if a final note had just been played

and the player, ashamed at being caught,
slammed shut the lid. Lucifer runs his scales,

his fingers curved above the Planck-length keys.
So many notes, the open and closed strings

hidden deep within the polished case . . .
the soundboard—all of Heaven—amplifies

each and every resonant frequency.
He thinks of his first lesson with the Word,

how stern her voice grew, counting off the time,
explaining as he shifted on the bench

that all there was was music, nothing else.
Practice, she would tell him, *it's important.*

He never figured out just what she meant.
Mostly, he liked to listen to *her* play,

and best of all when she thought no one heard.
He only learned one song of hers by heart,

a lullaby so sweet it made stars cry.
He plays it now to make his Father hurt.

ON THE NIGHT BEFORE
CREATION, LUCIFER DANCES
ON THE POINT OF A NEEDLE

Lucifer counts and takes a deep breath,
then steps out, partnerless, onto the stage
of the needle with which God embroiders the stars.
Nobody knows it's the end of an age —

he makes up a lover and gives her a name,
and pictures the solar wind blowing her hair
as they twirl in their huge, paradoxical gym.
She loves every minute. She says he has flair.

The angels can't help it, it looks like such fun —
they fold back their wings, and bow and join in.
But Lucifer doesn't much notice the crowd.
Her head's on his shoulder, just under his chin.

He dances and dances, until he grows tired,
then stops — but now, nobody is there.
The angels have gone. The dance floor has shrunk
to a pinprick of light, upon which he's speared

in the glare of God's gaze. The music is through.
Then the needle starts moving. *I have work to do.*

II

THE FIRST DAYS

1

Lucifer followed his Father to the edge
where Heaven stopped and nothingness began,
and saw the usual blank had been replaced
with varied forms of cruelty and dark:

here, balls of hot gas consuming themselves;
there, immense rocks colliding with their brothers.
What do you think of that one? asked his Father,
pointing towards one orb within the void.

Lucifer shrugged. *I guess it looks all right.*
When God his Father laughed, it was not kind.
It's terrible! He snorted. *Are you blind?*
But look at this. And God himself flew down
to that world's waters, and with a flourish cried
Let there be light! There was. And it was good—

not so bright or pure as that of Heaven,
but certainly much better than the gloom.
And in that light his Father swam the waves
while from above the cold rain pounded down.

Lucifer grew impatient. *What's the point?*
God came back to the surface with a frown.
What is the point? He spat. *What is the point?*
As I have thought, so shall it come to pass!

So shall it stand! Lucifer rolled his eyes.
He could not take his Father in these moods,
the *shalls* and *shall nots* coming thick and fast.
But then a sky appeared between the waters,
and blue it was, and full of God's new light.
The rain had stopped and gathered into clouds

3

and Lucifer's friends among the angels came
to sit upon them, bright wings folded up.
And God said to His audience, *Watch this,*
then brought the land from underneath the deep.

Such desolation none of them had seen,
the waste of rock like waves that did not move
except where chasms opened with a groan
or pockmarks on the surface belched up flames.

And from the ash and grime there sprouted forth
all kinds of growing things, and they were good,
though once again it seemed their colors paled
beside the greens of Heaven's massive trees.
But still the angels clapped . . . it was their call
to offer praise for everything He did,

even when what He did was not impressive.
But God perceived their mood, and tried to please.
He took the moon and hung it on the Earth.
He took the Earth and hung it on the sun.

And then God took a mountain in His hands
and spun the planet like a child's top,
so that the sun and moon changed their positions,
and unlike Heaven, one could see and feel

time as it passed, one hour at a time.
And as the days turned into night and back,
Lucifer noticed something he thought strange.
Father, he interrupted, *Why is it*
that as the days go by, the plants stop growing,
and crumble into dirt, and do not rise?

5

And God his Father answered, *They are dying,*
and said no more, but with a gesture formed
the fish and birds, who like the quiet plants
fell into ruin once their days were done—

the end of these was not so gentle, though.
Pain was in their movements. Their living flesh
crawled with worms that ate them from within.
And God saw this, and said that it was good,

and in its mercy darkness came to Earth
and hid the trembling of the host that watched.
But Lucifer shone too bright—he could not hide
the pall he felt at what was being done.
Why make their time so short? Why make the worms
to crawl their flesh? Why make this flesh at all

6

if you won't make it last the way we last?
The sun came up before his Father answered,
and in that light God called upon the Earth
to bring forth creatures, one after the next,

who grew and multiplied and slew each other.
And Lucifer was sick to smell the blood
that soaked the ground, and sick to see his Father
bending His smile to breathe in each fresh kill.

But there was one among them who was strange,
and in his features looked a lot like God.
Tell me, Father, what do you call that one?
And God rose to the height where they all sat
and put His feet up on a puff of cloud.
That animal is Man, the Lord began.

It is for Men that I have made all this.
Not for their pleasure, no. They are for mine.
And if they pass my tests, they will earn Heaven.
If they fail—well, that's where Hell comes in.

Lucifer gazed on the men. They made him sad,
for though they looked like Father, they were wretched.
The dirt of all creation covered them.
Cold cut through them, and in the sun they burned.

They died. And though they had not learned to speak
Lucifer could hear the lamentations
the living made, knowing they would fall.
You laid the streets of heaven. They make sense.
But nothing here makes any sense to me.
What kinds of tests will these poor things be given?

God grinned and put His arm around His son.
I knew that you were going to ask that question.
Do not despair. I would not leave you out
of all the plans that I've designed for Man.

Although they look like us, all these are flawed,
and full of lust and malice, sloth and spite.
Once they've mastered every kind of sin
I'll send you down to be their sacrifice . . .

all you have to do is let them kill you,
and then I'll bring you right back up to me.
Those who die believing you were mine
will join us here for all eternity.
Those who don't believe will burn and burn.
These are, of course, the broad strokes — there is more.

9

Lucifer stared at God, then turned away:
That is the worst idea I've ever heard.
He spoke no other word unto his Father,
but threw himself face first down to the world.

III

VERTIGO

Lucifer tries to stand . . . but no.
After a youth
on Heaven's perfect plane,

the terrible curve of the Earth
reduces him.
It is better to sit,

ringed round by the queasy angels.
They hide their eyes
beneath their shaking wings—

the work of having a body
exhausts them here.
He does not speak to them—

he does not, for years, even think.
The days and nights
spin past, the clamorous world

grinding its dizzying circles . . .
it steadies him
to know they will not last.

THE TREE

Lucifer wandered long to reach the Gate
where the Cherubim stood, their swords of fire
flickering in the desert wind. So lost

had he been in his thoughts . . . but now he saw
his angels were not there. He was alone.
He thought of turning back—the Garden's beauty

troubled him. What little order existed
was rough-edged, the work of hasty toil . . .
mostly, though, things just grew. Only the path

seemed maintained—like any alley in Heaven
if one kept his gaze on the ground. And so
Lucifer walked, the strangeness of Creation

all around him, but beneath his sore feet
something, at least, of home. How awful then
to hear that grunting speech—the man and woman

and Serpent, their uncomely mortal voices
barking with joy at something they had found.
What was that phrase the Word once used of man?

Created in the image of his Father.
A *metaphor*, Lucifer guessed. *Just listen
to how they chew! Even the angels had*—

then Lucifer raised his eyes, and beheld there
the path around the three all feather-strewn,
and the limbs of the Tree of Life weighed low

with the heads of his angels. And the Serpent
was in the branches, tossing that grim fruit
to the starving man and woman, who did eat.

Lucifer fled the Garden, kept his distance
from the blades of those at the Gate. The first
sacrifice had been made . . . and that accomplished,

the Lord removed the humans from that place,
burned the flowers down and plowed them under,
then whispered to His Serpent, *Do your worst.*

THE FLOOD

Lucifer backstrokes the deluge.
Far below, schools of perplexed fish

meander human streets. The calm
is deep. The only sound

is the crying of sparrows
as they fall, exhausted,

into the new seas. He stays away
from the awful boat

where 4,000 kinds of mammal
shit and whinny, the upper deck

where 9,000 species of bird
squawk, pecking each others' eyes

for space to sleep—
its bulk on the empty horizon

eclipses the sun. Lucifer
swims, avoiding the reek

of God's mercy, the ribbon of color
arcing the sky. But its shadow

marches triumphant
on all that floats past—

bits of cloth, lengths of wood,
the rickety crafts built in haste

by the laggard repentant.
The faces of livestock,

open-eyed. The faces
of infants, refusing to sink,

their wickedness punished at last.

THE BURNING BUSH

How Lucifer suffered the cold
of the lack of God . . . but here,

finally, was light and heat,
and so he could not resist—

he sat upon a rock
and warmed his hands, watching

as at the Lord's bidding
the human thrust his fist

into his heart, whereupon it died,
then pressed it in again

to make it live. *You
will obey*, the Fire explained,

*because I have made you to know
that you are nothing.* The flames

flickered and ceased, and all at once
the limbs which had not burned

fell into ash, a smoke
of sap and flesh. Again

Lucifer's spirit was chilled. Again
the human plunged his hands

inside his heart, each in turn,
so that whenever one had life

the other was pale. And Lucifer
was curious, well-versed

in every pain except for this —
Brother, he asked, *which*

do you prefer? Moses scowled . . .
Were you not listening? To Him,

they are the same. And then he fell
and covered his face with char . . .

He says they are the same,
and so they are.

TABLETS OF STONE

Oh look, here comes another one,
stumbling down a mountain
with shocked-white hair

and stone tablets chiseled with laws.
Lucifer shakes his head.
Another one . . .

these men walk a planet of stones,
each last pebble inscribed
in a clear hand

with verses too lengthy to speak
in the span of a life.
Can't men read them?

Would they, if they could? He wishes
the Word were here, her songs
not etched on sand

but in the air, for all to hear.
Wherever she has gone,
she's singing still,

Lucifer has to believe it.
In the meantime, he hums.
When prophets come,

shouting and tearing their clothing,
he goes into the hills.
When he returns

how discouraged his neighbors are
to see him approaching
without a beard

or bad news, in clean clothing, glad
to be home and waving
his empty hands.

THE TEMPTATION OF LUCIFER

Lucifer went to the desert
and grew his beard out long

and dressed in rags.
To eat, he had only the air . . .

to drink he had nothing
but sand. And after forty days

he saw a tent, and in its shade
a table laden with food,

and seated upon a stool
his younger brother, Jesus,

who called to him. *This task
is not so difficult—look,*

*here is food, and here is drink
prepared for the princes of the Kingdom.*

But Lucifer did not eat,
for though his stomach groaned

he knew the flesh of men
was what he smelled, and saw

that all around them
Hell gaped open. *Where*

is my brother, Lucifer asked.
Satan snickered

as he vanished from that place,
and Lucifer noticed

a plate of bones
picked clean,

and heard from within the tent
a sickly whimper.

Lucifer carried his brother
away from the wasteland

and back to the city of men.
Why are we here,

Jesus sighed. *What am I doing?*
Lucifer could not say.

They talked for a while
of Heaven, their favorite sights

in the Kingdom they had lost . . .
Why don't we just go back,

Jesus mumbled. *Why stay here
among devils and men? Father*

would understand. But neither
set his foot upon the stair

that appeared before them,
although it shone. *Soon enough,*

thought Jesus. *Never again,*
thought he who had no home.

THE PIGS

And after Jesus fled upon his boat,
the poor whose lives depended on the swine
ran down into the sea, to save the herd
that Legion, laughing, drove into the waves.
There they found the pigs upon the water,
not drowned or drowning or even in distress,
but swimming gaily, snapping after fish.
And seeing this, the men were full of wonder.
And seeing them, the swine were full of mirth . . .
they were many, the men were thin and few.
Enough!, the largest pig hissed to his fellows.
And to the men, he cooed, *You don't need ropes!*
We only had to rinse that Legion out.
Now that we're clean, we'll come back up the hill.
The men were tricked, and led them to the village
where Legion gulped their wine and pissed their beds,
two thousand strong and ready to ascend.
The men were whipped and made to till the fields . . .
their wives, enslaved . . . their children taught to squeal.
And after all this time, the swine still rule.
We do things their way, and listen as they snort
about the great things Jesus can do for *you*.

THE PARABLE OF THE DUST

One day it happened that the dust
lamented its dustness.
Friends, a mote cried,

we outnumber even the flies!
A second speck replied,
When the waves fail,

there we are, where always we were.
Show me one ray of light,
shouted a third,

where a thousand of us don't dance!
Show me the empty house
where we don't rule!

In Heaven, the Father of dust
heard all that was spoken.
The dust wanted

to be clean, to be respected,
to be a metaphor
not for the poor

or the dead, but the newborn child.
To be the mother's breast
swollen with milk,

wet at the tip . . . or better yet,
to be the womb itself.
The dust wanted

and wanted, and after a while
the Father of the dust
grew tired. *Listen,*

He began. And the dust listened.
But that was all He said,
for sleep had come

to the One who made dust the end
and not the beginning,
the omega,

the final word's far sibilant,
the hiss of the passing
of the last star . . .

When God awakes again, which dream
do you think He'll recall?
That oldest dream—

how it used to terrify Him—
where men beg for mercy?
Or the dust dream

where grit learns to speak? Already
He's grumbling, and rubbing
His stinging eyes . . .

Who made all this light? And these birds!
Remind me, angels—why
must these things sing?

The crown of thorns, yes. But not
the blood upon the cheek. The scourge,

yes, but not the bruise.
A stranger, Simon, bearing up the cross,

yes, but not the child trampled
by the crowd. The crowd,

yes, but not those who waited inside
for the shouting to end. Criminals,

one on either side . . . yes,
and on the ground, soldiers

dividing their clothes. And Lucifer
was there, well-known by those

closest in friendship to the Crucified—
along with them he wept, although he knew

all that was taking place, and what it meant . . .
Leave me out, he begged them,

of anything you write about this day.
The day made night, the temple curtain

torn, the dead walking. Yes, yes—
but Lucifer lifting wine

to his brother's lips? Or his song,
which only the dying could hear

for it came of the Kingdom?
No, nothing, nothing of his song.

It is finished. Yes.
Why have you forsaken me?

Yes. But his Father's answer?
Lost in the beating of breasts

and the rending of rocks,
the momentary hush

of the wind shocked still.
Among the living

none but Lucifer heard.
For reasons I can only guess

he refuses to talk.

For you are like their parent
              who is never pleased
   and they are like your parent
              who cannot stay angry

For you are like a child

For age after age
              they conceive you
   and despite the pain of birth
              they bring you forth

For they call you perfect
              though your hands are missing
   and though your heart does not beat
              they give you a name

For they remember you

For they hold you blameless
              in their sorrow
   though they were surely happiest
              before you arrived

For your identical twin
              they name Silence
   and when they feed Silence
              he grows

For they love Silence
              as they would have loved you
   even more perhaps
              as old age comes

and they forget
                    the sound of your cry
        and where the exact spot was
                    they spread your ashes

and how those ashes
                    tasted
        when the wind blew them
                    into their mouths

Father in their dreams
                    they worry still
        perhaps it is you
                    who lives among them

and not Silence
                    after all
        mistakes happen
                    after all

how would anyone know

and the midwives
                    forgive them
        forgive them
                    were only human

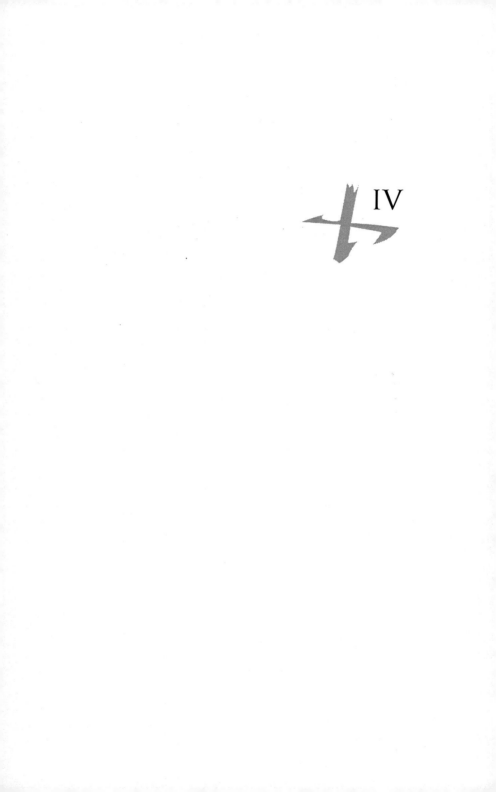

IV

Tremble, earth, at the absence of God
which turns standing water to desert

and desert to sand, sand to atoms,
atoms to particles, particles

to theory, a human hand grasping
for faith it will not call faith. Tremble

at faith, which turns the quark to nothing,
the atom to nothing and the earth

to a test. Tremble to be tested.
Be untested and tremble. Have faith

and tremble all the same—you cannot
stop trembling, it is what you're made of,

each cell, every last shimmering nerve—
the more you hold still your hand, the more

it wants to shake. How little it takes
to reduce you to the desert you are,

a thing that burns, with faith or without,
the fountains of your eyes becoming sand.

LUCIFER'S WINDOW

There once was a time of miracles.
You never knew what you'd see

when you lifted the shade—
a pillar of fire, a river

turned to blood, enough hard rain
to drown the continent—every day

the divine made commonplace,
the hand of God so close

you could read His palm.
God spoke to His creation

when He despised it.
Now that man is forgiven

there's not much to say.
Lucifer watches, anyway . . .

as old as he sometimes feels
the world seems young, always full

of absurd fires, winds
that refuse to calm. And man

still entertains—there's one now,
taking his trash to the curb. And another . . .

every Thursday, the garbage truck
crashes their mortal dreams

and for just a while
the whole block stinks

like Vengeance, the air thick with flies
and rot. It is August,

and the street is so hot
you could burn an offering,

though no one will think to do it.
Why should they

when there is no wrath to appease?
The truck groans by

like Aaron's lucky goat,
taking their filth past the corner

and into the wild.

LUCIFER FEEDS THE BILLIONS
AND BILLIONS

One by one, the hungry and tired
speak to the flood-lit air

their urgent needs — prayers
like any others, though these are heard

In Thirty Seconds or Less!
by the sullen, pimpled kid

whose calling it is to attend
the tiled confessional

of the first drive-thru window.
And at the second, Lucifer

answers them, one and all,
with a grin and a bright *Come Again*

even at the end of his shift.
How long has it been? He was here

when the sign read *Millions,*
then *Hundreds of Millions,*

then billions counted one by one
until one day, mankind

stopped counting. The cars
come and come, each door

with its *cinéma vérité*—
a man strikes his child so hard

her lip drips red. A woman's mouth
works the driver's lap—not once

does she look up. But mostly
the scenes are the same, as if faces

were the mass-produced foodstuff
and he the customer, starving,

reaching an eager hand
for the bagful of grease. And yet

none of these lacks a name—
He who formed each from the dust

has known from the first breath of life
which faces want fries, the smell

of their engine, the date
on every coin and crumpled bill.

But for now, it's break time. Lucifer
punches his card, and ponders these things

in his heart. How cold the car is
in the crowded, starless lot. How sore

his feet are. How his stomach growls.

PSALM

Happy are those
          who keep their trust
     in you, Father,

for they are like trees
          planted
     between the long rows

of parking lots
          in suburban strip malls,
     ringed round

by brick or cobblestone
          and twice a week
     watered

by Hope, that aging dropout
          who against all odds
     got clean

and is grateful
          even punctual
     singing

as he sweeps
          spent cigarettes
     off the pavement.

How easy faith is
          for the faithful . . .
     when their boughs

grow wild
                    he trims them.
          When winter comes

their nakedness
                    is clothed with lights.
          Father

I envy these trees
                    the stakes and cables
          that hold them true

and the way
                    on a single spring day
          they all seem

to blossom at once.
                    Here in the forest
          the darkness comes

so early
                    and those smallest of angels
          the birds

stay just half the year.
                    When visitors
          walk beneath us

they respect us
                    too much . . .
          how rarely

are their loves scratched
                    into our bark!
          Lord

when you come
in the driest week
of our driest summer

remember
your bad habits.
Bring your best knife

and your cigarettes.
Into our midst
drop your match.

Lucifer knew his wife. Nine months later,
the kindly doctor cuts her belly open

and lifts his daughter out into the light.
And after she's been held, and gazed upon,

and her name, for the first time, has been spoken,
the surgeon calls, *Hey, Papa, have a look!*

A few feet down from his wife's smile, her life
lies open, as bloody as he'd imagined

and far more colorful, the womb's gray shell
gaping and empty, and all around it

her—not the face he loves, the sense of humor,
but the lurid orchard of the abdomen,

the fruit of Eden glistening as it rots.
Lucifer thinks of the angels, as simple

as paper dolls inside—and of his Father,
who changed His shape for lust or metaphor—

they take it all so lightly, having form.
But here are veins and their cargo, the spleen

and its moods. Here is that time-bomb gag-gift
the appendix, the furnace of the stomach

burning every death she shovels in.
One wrong touch could end her, even here,

but it's not death he fears. His daughter whimpers
as they wipe away her birth. *Hey Baby,*

the woman calls—and as he turns, his head
smacks hard on a lamp. *Babe, am I pretty?*

she jokes, exhausted. *You're gorgeous,* he smiles—
and for her sake, reminds himself to bleed.

LUCIFER'S BEGINNING
POETRY WORKSHOP

Lucifer loves the beginners.
He loves how their hands shake

as they pull their Xeroxed drafts
from their untattered folders,

and the way, bright as they are,
it takes them two months to learn

to pass those poems to their peers
in an organized fashion. It reminds him

of creation, the galactic mess
spinning from his Father's hands—

hands beyond holding, as white
as starlight, unblemished

but for long-bitten nails.
He likes to read the descriptions

of his students' fathers' hands, huge
and calloused with labor, as if

they'd done something new
beneath the sun. He savors

their familiar emotions,
the familiar deserted woods

where each walks a well-beaten path
they insist is less-traveled.

Give up, he tells each one,
Try law, medicine, the clergy—

even God had the modesty,
after making this first failed world,

to take a rest. But in truth,
he applauds how they go on,

how week after week
the dreadful drafts are brought forth . . .

Lucifer reads them all
and calls them good.

I praise you, O Father,
>though why you need my praise
>I cannot imagine —

what could I possibly say
>to augment your greatness?
>How could the silence of my tongue

diminish you?
>Yet you demand it,
>created a world of voices

to sing out your name.
>What happened to you?
>Were your parents cruel?

Were you teased on the playground?
>Are you short?
>How hard it is to need

a needy god.
>Still, I sing.
>You hear, I suppose,

though what it seems like to you
>I can only guess . . .
>so many billions of mouths

all sobbing your name.
>How reluctantly
>you must attend

to the clamor of church bells.
    How weary you must be
    of the call to prayer.

Let us compromise
    for both our sakes—
    you allow me

to keep silent,
    and I will consent
    not to speak.

LUCIFER VISITS HOME

It seemed to make sense
at the time—*he*

was the prodigal son, who was dead
then alive, lost and then found,

and if he came home
to the Kingdom, safe and sound

and begging redemption,
his aging Dad would rejoice

to see his face. So glad
was Lucifer's heart, turning the key

in the closed garage, breathing
in, in . . .

◆

The Gate is ajar, creaking
on its starry hinge. No other song

meets his call. No robe
is wrapped round his shoulders,

no fatted calf killed—
he wanders the streets, passing

the boarded stores. Here and there,
through a locked window,

a glimpse of furniture draped
in dusty sheets. The gutters

littered with feathers
and unanswered prayers.

Not even a note
on the fridge . . .

◆

It was, of course, an accident
he explains to his grateful wife

and the EMTs. The car
will need to be looked at

right away—he'd only just
turned the key, and then . . .

And because they stare
with such longing, he describes

the joy in the many voices
of his lost beloved, the warmth

of the next world's welcome,
the light of the light of all lights.

THE PARABLE OF THE BEES

Listen: beside a cherry tree in bloom
Lucifer parked his car. When he returned

the day had grown hot, and the car's dark hood
was dappled with pale blossoms. And honeybees —

each as big as the bud with which he grappled —
clung to the flowers, drunken with sweetness.

And there were some among them who were dead,
scorched from too much frolicking on the steel,

the blossoms that entombed them baked to gold.
Lucifer took the wheel. One at a time,

flowers slipped over the windshield, and with them
their small lovers, until a semi's wake

threw them into the air. Lucifer watched
in the mirror . . . before they hit the pavement,

he was gone. This is the Kingdom of Heaven . . .
not bees nor sweetness. Not heat. You are lofted

by God's swift passage. How fast He drives
away from us. How many sharp turns He takes.

LUCIFER'S INSOMNIA

No, not today—the sun rises
the way it always does,

and Lucifer's mortal lover
stretches her arms

as he pretends again to stretch his own.
Should it not have ended

by this time? The woman
is his wife, his thousandth,

but the core of the world
still burns in its young skin,

the nightful of stars
the same, more or less,

as the day he fell.
The woman, too, is young,

and though the end
is nothing that she thinks of,

he stays awake each night
to watch her perish . . .

a cell here, a hair there,
a new line at the eyes

that will not wash.
Rise up, my love,

Lucifer says,
until the day arrives

that she does not.
How still she is

upon the spinning earth.
How still the earth is

in its place among the stars.
How still the stars are, forgotten

in the mind of God.
The hot sun sets and sets.

Lucifer forgets nothing,
counting their names

in the darkness
he makes himself see . . .

for every night they have,
he has all night.

LUCIFER AT THE END OF DAYS

How cold it is, now that the stars have died
and each last speck of cosmic grime has sped
unto the edges of imagination,
the nearest thing now infinitely far.

Lucifer wanders, still. It's been so long
there is no bit of Earth he has not touched
a thousand times. He walks the frozen seas,
recalling the boats of man, the funny lights

that spun in coastal towns to guide them home.
What did they call those lights? Where were those towns?
The waves of ice are deep; he can't see through
to where those cities lie. He misses man—

there's one he still recalls especially,
a boy so frightened of death he lay awake
night after night. *What if there is no God?*
he asked each page of his journal, *What if*

we only die? But God exists, or did.
And now that all His plans have reached perfection
it's almost as it was before the start.
Silence and dark. *What if,* Lucifer sighs,

surprised to hear a voice, even his own.
He'd give up half his light to cast a glow
on any living thing. But it's too cold.
Nothing lives. Whatever it is he does,

it isn't living, quite. Has never been.
The urge strikes him as odd, almost comic—
to go to sleep. Just what would be the point,
here at the end? And yet the living slept—

they could not live without it. More and more
the idea charms him. What dreams might he have?
How long might he rest? And if the dark day
breaks, what will have changed? He lays himself down

but seems in the next moment to awaken.
My son, my son, murmurs the Word, shaking
his shoulder, smiling and frowning at once.
Where has your Father gone? What has He done?

NOTES ON THE POEMS

Many of the poems make reference to, or steal directly from, certain Biblical passages. While some of the references are quite obvious and well known, others may be more obscure, so most are listed here.

"The Birth of Lucifer": John, Chapter 1.

"Lucifer's Dog": Revelation, Chapter 4.

"The Departure of the Word": The description of the Word's voice as "still, small" comes from Kings 19:12.

"The First Days": Genesis, Chapters 1 and 2.

"The Tree": Genesis, Chapter 3.

"The Flood": Genesis, Chapters 6-8.

"The Burning Bush": Exodus, Chapters 3-4.

"The Temptation of Lucifer": The story of the temptation of Jesus is told in Matthew, Chapter 4, Mark, Chapter 1, and Luke, Chapter 4.

"The Pigs": The story of Legion is told in Mark, Chapter 5 and Luke, Chapter 8.

"Gospel": The crucifixion story is told in all four of the Gospels, with slightly different details; elements from each are combined here.

"Psalm (Tremble, earth)": Psalm 114.

"Lucifer's Window": Leviticus, Chapter 16.

"Lucifer Feeds the Billions and Billions": The story of the loaves and fishes is found in Matthew, Chapter 14, Mark, Chapter 6, Luke, Chapter 9, and John, Chapter 6. The phrase "ponders these things in his heart" is adapted from Luke 2:19.

"Lucifer's Fear": The euphemism in the first line is borrowed from Genesis 4:1 and 4:17, and other Genesis elements appear later in the poem.

"Lucifer's Beginning Poetry Workshop": The phrase "something new beneath the sun" is borrowed from Ecclesiastes. The final lines, of course, refer to Genesis, Chapter 1.

"Lucifer Visits Home": The story of the prodigal son is told in Luke, Chapter 15.

"Lucifer's Insomnia": The quote in line 22 is from Song of Solomon: 2:10.